The Golden Age of Baghdad

Written by Richard Platt
Illustrated by Andrea Rossetto

T0382013

Contents

Collins

The finest city

The world's biggest and finest city 1,100 years ago was not Paris, London or New York. It was the desert city of Baghdad in what is now Iraq.

Baghdad in 900 CE was a glamorous, glorious place of civilisation and **scholarship**. It had fine, marble-walled palaces, lush parks and gardens, and glittering temples. Its huge libraries stored and preserved all the earth's knowledge. The city's **scholars** were the best in the world. In its bustling markets, merchants and shoppers bought **exotic goods** from as far away as China. Families strolled in its wide streets, which were swept spotlessly clean.

Baghdad's glory is all the more amazing when compared with other places. Many European cities were small, **squalid** and unhealthy. Warfare and political rivalry made life miserable. Travel was slow and dangerous. There was little trade, and scholarship and education were primitive. Only in China were there cities that rivalled Baghdad in size or magnificence.

Today Baghdad's past glory, glamour and achievement are forgotten or ignored, but they shouldn't surprise us. The city was simply the twinkling centrepiece of an enormously powerful empire that dominated the known world.

The Islamic world

Baghdad owed its fame and wealth to religion and conquest.
Three centuries earlier, a **prophet** called Muhammad
had gathered around him a band of faithful followers.
Called Muslims (an Arabic word meaning "those who
surrender to God"), they helped Muhammad spread
his religion of Islam, and its holy book, the Quran,
throughout Arabia.

This vast, hot, roughly triangular land was the centre of
the Islamic world. But Muhammad's followers had influence
and power far beyond Arabia's shores on the Gulf, the Red
Sea and the Indian Ocean.

Muslim warriors began their
conquests just two years
after Muhammad's death.

After Muhammad's death in 632 CE, new leaders, called "caliphs", continued his work, spreading Islam to the west and to the north. In little more than a century, they controlled all of North Africa, Spain and Portugal. In the north, the **caliphate** had spread to the Caspian Sea, and in the east it reached almost to China.

These lands were quickly **conquered** because their rulers had been weakened by fighting amongst themselves and because their people were often discontent. When they faced opposition, advancing Muslim armies won battles because they were fast, well organised, and because their shared religion helped soldiers fight the enemy together.

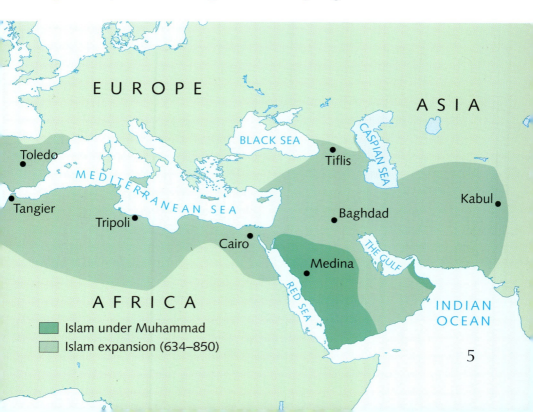

EUROPE

ASIA

BLACK SEA

Toledo

Tiflis

CASPIAN SEA

MEDITERRANEAN SEA

Tangier

Kabul

Tripoli

Baghdad

Cairo

THE GULF

Medina

RED SEA

AFRICA

INDIAN OCEAN

Islam under Muhammad
Islam expansion (634–850)

The jewel in the centre

Revolution shook the vast caliphate in the middle of the 8th century, kicking out the old rulers. A new **dynasty** called the Abbasids took power, and the caliph, Al-Manṣūr wanted a new capital city.

He chose to build it on the Tigris River in what is now Iraq. There were practical reasons for his choice: the river could supply the city with ample water; the Tigris was also a transport highway, bringing trade goods up from the Persian Gulf; and just 15 kilometres to the south the **Euphrates** River joined the Tigris, bringing ships from Syria.

But it was also a political decision. The old capital was Damascus in Syria, but support for the Abbasids was stronger in Iraq. Also, the Abbasids had **allies** in nearby Persia (now Iran) and relied on Persian families for important government jobs.

Al-Manṣūr chose the spot for the city himself, after searching along the river. Stopping at an ancient Persian village, he announced, "This is a good place … Here's the Tigris, with nothing between us and China, and on it arrives all that the sea can bring …"

Al-Manṣūr imagined the city as a vast circle. This was a traditional shape for the towns of Persia, and very different from the grid-like pattern of cities in the ancient civilisations of Greece and Rome. The caliph chose Persian architects to design the city, too.

Building the city

Al-Manṣūr brought in 100,000 craftsmen from Syria, Persia and Babylonia to build Baghdad. They created an extraordinary and magnificent city. They began construction in 762 CE by sketching the outline of the city on the ground, first in ash, and then with flaming torches that lit up the desert night in a circle of fire.

This ring became the foundation of the city's outer wall. A deep water-filled ditch surrounded it to protect the wall against attack. And within the outer wall was a second higher circular wall.

This inner wall was 32 metres thick at the base and 27 metres in height. Visitors to the city entered through four gateways. At night, these were blocked by iron gates, each so vast that it took several guards to close each one.

At the very heart of the city, craftsmen created a magnificent **mosque**, and another circular wall. This protected Al-Manṣūr's palace.

The city was built almost entirely from mud-brick, because there was no stone nearby. Rain was rare, and mud-brick was the traditional building material. Its uniform colour made all streets look similar, but stepping through a door changed everything. Inside, buildings were richly decorated with colourful tiles.

When the city was complete, after four years of labour, it was known as the Round City, or City of Manṣūr.

Mosques, palaces and markets

In 900 CE, Baghdad was very different from the city Al-Manṣūr had built. It was much bigger, taking three hours to walk across. As soon as the circular walls were complete, building work had started on **suburbs**. The city had also been damaged by warfare. In an attack nearly a century earlier, giant catapults had pounded holes in some of the walls.

Despite this damage, the city was still magnificent with impressive palaces and grand houses. One visitor wrote that "... these mansions were lavishly decorated, and hung with beautiful tapestry of silk. The rooms were furnished with luxurious couches, costly tables, unique Chinese vases and gold and silver ornaments ..."

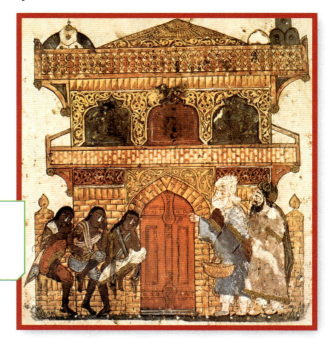

Paintings of fine palaces decorated Arab story collections.

10

Everywhere the roofs and towers of mosques broke up Baghdad's skyline: storytellers bragged that the city had 35,000 mosques. Inside, they were beautifully decorated with marble and coloured glazed tiles.

Baghdad was also a place of business. In the bustling merchants' suburb of Karkh, you could buy almost anything. Every trade had its own market, called a "suk": dates, cotton, horses, gold, sweets, hay, weapons, metalwork, clothes, jewels and money all had their own markets.

Spice stalls in today's traditional suks are little different from those in Baghdad 11 centuries ago.

Greening the desert

After marvelling at luxurious palaces, visitors gasped at fields around the city. Baghdad was a rare splash of green in the desert. In the summer growing season, temperatures reached 40 degrees centigrade and no rain fell, yet Baghdad's plants were never **parched**.

Gardens provided cool, shady places for scholars to talk.

It was river water that kept the crops green. Much of it came from the Tigris. But the Euphrates was a metre or so higher than the river it joined, so – with a lot of digging – farmers could drain its water towards the city. Where gravity alone was not enough to move the water, farmers lifted it with machines such as the "sāqiyah", a chain of pots turned by animals.

Water in Baghdad was so plentiful that it wasn't just used for farming. It fed lush green gardens bursting with leafy **fragrance**. Gardens **enchanted** Arab people: the Persians even had a special style of poem, the "rawḍīya", praising them.

There was a serious side to gardening: Baghdad's plots preserved rare and tender plant varieties. A 10th-century caliph planted his Baghdad courtyard with sour orange trees brought from India.

Some Baghdad gardens used water on its own to surprise visitors: three Persian brothers called the Banū Mūsā described in their *Book of Tricks* how to make automatic fountains that squirted ever-changing patterns of jets and sprays.

Mud-brick comfort

Nothing remains of the houses of ancient Baghdad: they crumbled to dust long ago. But from ruins elsewhere, we can guess what they were like. They were built of bricks moulded from mud and strengthened with plant fibres. Thick walls with tiny windows kept out searing noon heat, and stored it to warm the family inside during cold desert nights.

Many ordinary houses in the city had a single storey; steps led up to a flat roof where the family slept under the stars on the hottest nights. But a few may have been taller: elsewhere in Arabia, mud-brick apartment blocks rose as high as 30 metres.

Houses for all but the wealthiest were very simple. They had only a few rooms. In a larger house, one of these would be reserved for women, who under the rules of Islam could mix only with men who were family members. In smaller homes, a curtain hid women from male visitors.

Houses lacked indoor plumbing and kitchens, and the only furnishings were mats, carpets and cushions. Much family activity happened in courtyards around which houses clustered: here people cooked and ate, and entertained their guests.

In Shibam, Yemen, builders have created skyscrapers from mud-brick.

Everyday life

Hospitality and generosity are an Arab tradition, so families treated visitors to the finest food they could afford. Wealthy households served true banquets; even the poor tried to greet guests with meat dishes, and the produce of the farms around the city. The **irrigated** fields provided fresh green vegetables, olives, grapes, bananas, melons and coconuts.

When they had no guests, poorer families ate some of these things, but chickpea porridge, bread, treacle, pickles, olives and fish made up more of their diet, and the poorest ate locusts. Women cooked most of this food on open fires; houses lacked ovens, so a communal bakehouse cooked bread and baked dishes.

People squatted on the floor to eat at low tables, as they still do in the Arab world.

Clothing

To protect themselves from the powerful desert sun, everyone wore loose-fitting clothes that covered most of the body. Religious rules required that women cover their faces and hair in public, but it's possible that only wealthier women did this all the time. A face-covering veil made movement difficult, and women of poorer families may not have worn one for housework or farm work. Likewise, for hard labour, men stripped off, wearing just a **loincloth** in the fields.

For Baghdad's citizens, it was traditional to wash before five-times daily prayers, and the city's 27,000 bath houses meant that nobody had to travel far to scrub and soak.

poorer men working in the fields

Men and women

Public life in Baghdad was a very male affair. Women took no part in government or business. When men weren't working, they relaxed in male company. Women were expected to remain in the home.

Even there, women mixed only with men who were close relatives: when entertaining male guests at home, men expected their wives to cook and serve food – then disappear.

So how did women spend their time when they were apart from men? If they were rich, they had servants and enslaved people to wait on them, and they enjoyed themselves with female friends and relatives.

Poor women had a harder time. As well as doing housework and childcare, they fetched water, and dried animal dung to burn as fuel. They also earned money by spinning and weaving at home.

Women could spin and weave at home without being seen by men.

Separation continued even at the mosque. Men were expected to pray there, but women more often prayed at home. If they did attend the mosque, they worshipped in a separate room.

The separation between men and women was an ancient tradition, and ruled by verses in the holy Quran.

Women sat in a different part of a mosque than men.

Children and school

Unlike adults, young boys and girls of Baghdad mixed freely. They played together in ways that have hardly changed today: with toy animals, balls and puppet theatres. But when games ended and it was time for school, boys and girls had different experiences.

Boys attended the mosque to pray and to study. A famous book of the time advised: "Teach your children to pray when they reach seven, and when they are ten, beat them if they neglect it."

Boys' education was religious: they learnt to read, recite and memorise the Quran. Only when they were older did they study other subjects such as Mathematics.

Classrooms were simple: the teacher sat on a mat, with the class in front of him in a half circle. Paper was costly, so students wrote on washable pieces of wood using a pen made from a reed.

A few girls studied in this way, but, more often, girls got very little education. Their parents taught them to pray, but concentrated on practical skills such as needlework and embroidery. Only in wealthy families did girls learn to read and write.

In the poorest of homes, education for either sex was impossible, for children were useful little workers: as toddlers they could scare birds from fields, and at seven years they were old enough to tend flocks of animals.

In the classroom scholars took turns to fan the teacher.

The Islamic Golden Age

Under the Abbasid dynasty that had founded Baghdad,
it had grown into the world's richest and biggest city.
But Baghdad had also become great in ways that you couldn't
count or measure. For just as the wealth of Baghdad – and
the whole Islamic world – had grown, so too had Arab
knowledge and scholarship.

The Islamic religion was one reason for this: the Quran
praised the value of learning and encouraged study.
Money helped, too. The growing wealth of the caliphate
allowed the government to sponsor study and to create new
places of learning.

There was also curiosity about the way the world worked,
and an interest in the writings of experts from the ancient
civilisations of Greece and Rome. In particular, Islamic scholars
read the works of Greek experts such as scientist Archimedes,
mathematician Euclid, and **philosopher** Aristotle.

Copies of their writings in the Greek language circulated
in the Arab world. In Europe, where very few people
spoke or read Greek, these important texts were forgotten
or destroyed.

This flowering of thought, education and culture has been called the Islamic Golden Age because the Arab scholars' achievements would remain the best in the world for three centuries.

Muslim scientists invented equipment and methods that are still used in modern laboratories.

23

Thirst for knowledge

Baghdad had been a centre of learning and scholarship almost since the city began. Its founder, Al-Manṣūr, was fascinated by the movements of the stars and planets, and by philosophy. In 771 CE, he encouraged Indian scholars to visit Baghdad. They brought with them new knowledge of mathematics and astronomy that was crucial to the study of science in the city.

Al-Manṣūr's encouragement of learning led to a growth in education that continued long after his lifetime: a visitor to the city four centuries later counted 30 colleges there.

New technology – paper

Al-Manṣūr had a new tool for spreading knowledge: paper. It was easier to make than the calfskin parchment used for writing in Europe, and lasted longer than papyrus, the reed paper of Egypt.

Paper's Chinese inventors jealously guarded the secret of its manufacture, but when a Muslim army defeated Chinese soldiers in 751 CE, they captured a papermaker. He taught them how to make filthy rags into crisp white pages.

Baghdad became such a famous centre for papermaking that one of the Greek words for paper was "bagdatixon".

Thanks to this cheap new writing material, the wisdom of Baghdad's cleverest scholars was copied, recorded and spread to the farthest corners of the Islamic world.

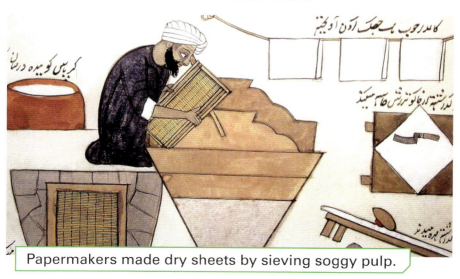

Papermakers made dry sheets by sieving soggy pulp.

The House of Wisdom

Caliph Al-Manṣūr put the vast wealth of the caliphate behind his scheme for education and study. He started a royal library and added to it space for scholars to work and for **scribes** to copy books – printing was not yet invented. Clerks and officials made sure that nothing distracted or disturbed these brainy experts.

This huge and ambitious scheme to **cultivate**, preserve and spread knowledge became known as the "House of Wisdom".

a scribe and a painter at work

The translation movement

Some of the work of the House of Wisdom was translation – writing Arabic versions of foreign-language books. The translators started with books written 1,000 years earlier in Greece, and with 400-year-old books from the Roman Empire. Everyone respected the writers of these ancient books as the wisest and most knowledgeable people in history. Soon translations of ancient Indian writings were added to the library.

The translators who did this valuable work were as famous and glamorous as rock stars are today – the best were paid in gold the same weight as the books they translated.

Arabic translation of a Greek science text

The first universities

Respect for knowledge and the encouragement of study spread far beyond Baghdad, to the whole Islamic world. Some 4,500 kilometres to the west in the city of Fez (now in Morocco), teaching began in 859 CE at the world's first university. Called Al Quaraouiyine, it opened more than two centuries before Europe's first university in Bologna. Another university opened in Cairo in 970 CE.

Baghdad didn't have its own university, Al-Nizamiyya, until a century later, but this quickly became the world's largest. These universities started as places to study Islam, but they soon added other non-religious subjects.

Quaraouiyine university in Fez, Morocco

Libraries

Like modern universities, each had a library at its centre. Some had many thousands of books, and as more books were translated, libraries grew to house them. Baghdad's caliphs also had their own libraries: at the end of the 10th century, the library of Al-Aziz had 40 rooms full of books, including 18,000 on science.

By comparison, European libraries were small and neglected. Most were in cathedrals and monasteries, and were little more than locked chests containing a few hundred books.

In this library, books are stacked in niches in the wall.

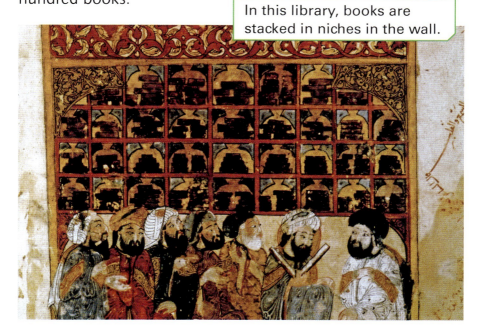

The first scientists

Scholars in Islamic universities studied ancient Greek texts about science, but then they did something **radically** new: they compared what they read with what they saw happening in the world. When the two didn't agree, they tried to create a better explanation – and then checked this with experiments. Today, we call this process the "scientific method" and it's a test all scientific knowledge must pass before it's accepted as fact.

The books that scientists of Baghdad and elsewhere in the Islamic world wrote about their work would later spread their knowledge to Europe and beyond.

a statue of Al-Khwarizmi, situated near the old walls of the city of Khiva, Uzbekistan

Al-Khwarizmi

Amongst the most famous of Baghdad's scientists was Muhammad ibn Musa Al-Khwarizmi. Born around 780 CE in the part of Persia that is now Uzbekistan, he became a researcher in the House of Wisdom, where he studied ancient Indian scientific books. He was amongst the world's greatest astronomers, and the tables he created to predict the positions of the sun and planets remained in use for 1,000 years. Al-Khwarizmi also wrote several books about mathematics and **calculation**. One of these introduced readers to the Indian way of writing numbers – including zero – that we use today and call "Arabic numerals".

Mathematics

Scholars in the House of Wisdom built on what they had learnt from Greek and Indian mathematicians to create powerful ways of understanding the world and solving problems.

Numbers

Arab experts spread knowledge of the 0–9 signs we use for counting and calculation today. The numbers slowly replaced the Roman numerals – I, V, X – that you still see on old clocks. The new system made calculations easy: with Roman numbers they were impossible without a squared board and counters.

Sums with 0–9 numbers (left) were easier and quicker than using the Roman counting board (right).

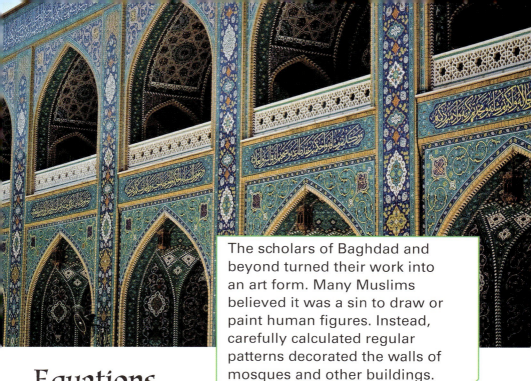

The scholars of Baghdad and beyond turned their work into an art form. Many Muslims believed it was a sin to draw or paint human figures. Instead, carefully calculated regular patterns decorated the walls of mosques and other buildings.

Equations

Al-Khwarizmi worked out how to solve problems with equations by writing numbers as symbols, such as letters, on either side of an equals sign. The name for algebra comes from the title of his book, *Kitab al-jabr wa'l-muqabala* (Restoring and Balancing).

The sine function

This number is the ratio of two sides of a triangle, and it's different for each angle. Sines were important because they allowed mathematicians to solve angle problems using sums, rather than drawing diagrams on paper.

Astronomy and timekeeping

Arab scholars studied the science of astronomy because the movements of the sun, moon, stars and planets tracked the changing hours and seasons. Time and date were important in religion: they told Muslims when to pray, and when to celebrate yearly festivals. People also believed that the planets' positions predicted the future – a mistaken superstition we now call astrology.

Greek and Indian knowledge of the stars was the starting point for Arab studies, but the astronomers in the House of Wisdom did much more than translate old books. They carefully checked what they read by observing the stars, measuring their positions, and timing when they rose and set.

They were encouraged by a caliph, Al-Mamun, who took a great interest in both astronomy and astrology. In 828 CE, he built an **observatory** in Baghdad. Two years later, Al-Khwarizmi published his famous star and planet tables.

In 900 CE, astronomer Al-Battani produced his own tables, and calculated the length of the year (the time it takes for the earth to go round the sun) with an error of just 150 seconds. This made calendars far more accurate:

Even without telescopes, astronomers learnt a lot about the stars by measuring the angles between them, and the times they rose and set.

the best European estimates were nearly 12 minutes wrong, which meant that people celebrated Christian festivals such as Christmas a day earlier every 128 years.

Technology

Baghdad's astronomers had no telescopes to look at the skies – these were 700 years in the future – but they did have instruments to help their observations. The most important of these was the astrolabe, a circular metal disc with pointers for measuring the angles of the stars. Astrolabes had many uses: their engraved surfaces were like calculators, showing everything from the time of sunrise to the direction to face when praying.

This part of the astrolabe shows different latitudes – how far something is to the north or south of the earth's equator.

this part of the astrolabe rotates

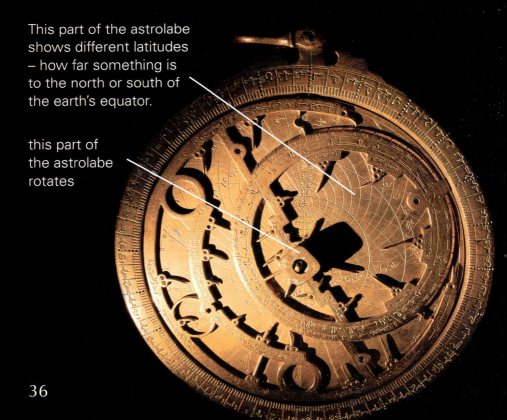

Astrolabes were so **ingenious**, powerful and **baffling** that when they reached Europe those who used them were sometimes accused of being **sorcerers**.

The makers of astrolabes used their engineering skills to create other miraculous machines. Perhaps the most important were mechanical clocks. From the 10th century onwards, engineers created **complex** clocks, powered by water, weights or flowing **mercury**. Some even displayed the positions of the sun, moon and planets, but more often they were used to show the time of prayers.

Not all technology had such serious aims: some was created for the amusement of the caliph or some other rich sponsor. For instance, the Banū Mūsā, the three Persian brothers who wrote the *Book of Tricks*, invented a robotic flute player, and a mysterious jar that squirted hot and cold water from a basin and from the mouth of a figure above it.

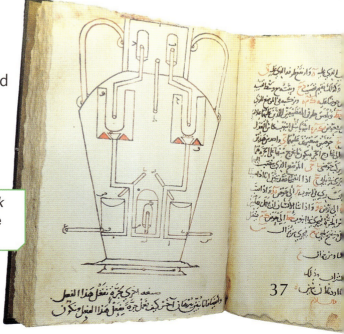

a page from the *Book of Tricks* showing one of the inventions

37

Medicine

If you fell ill in 900 CE, survival depended more on luck than on your doctor's skill. Like doctors everywhere, those in Baghdad believed that patients' star signs were as important as their **symptoms**. And the most popular treatment – draining off a patient's blood – was more likely to kill than cure. But in other ways, medical treatment in the Arab world was more advanced than in Europe. Hospitals and their patients were clean, **infectious** cases were separated from others, and doctors visited each patient regularly. Poppy juice, which contains the powerful painkiller morphine, eased patients' suffering.

As today, hospitals treated only the sickest patients in beds.

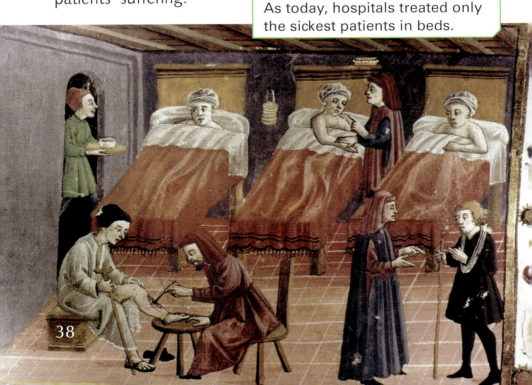

Rhazes

Muhammad ibn Zakariya Al-Razi – known to Europeans as "Rhazes" – has been called "the greatest physician of Islam and the Medieval Ages". Thirty-five years old in 900 CE, he's best known for the 224 books he wrote on medicine and other subjects. These included what we now call a home medical **manual**, and a book that showed for the first time that **smallpox** and measles were different diseases.

Rhazes became the chief doctor of Baghdad hospital. He chose where to build it by hanging raw meat in the city's streets, judging that the healthiest spot was where the meat stayed fresh for longest.

Rhazes wasn't just a doctor: he was a keen experimenter, and was the first to extract pure alcohol from wine.

Freedom and tolerance

Scholars, translators, scientists and thinkers of all nationalities and religions mixed freely together in Baghdad. Although the official religion was Islam, Christians, Hindus, Jews, **Zoroastrians**, **Sabeans** and **pagans** were all welcome, and this helped to bring about a rich exchange of knowledge and ideas.

Tolerance for non-Muslims, called "dhimmi", was an Islamic tradition, and was one of the reasons why the Arab conquests had been swift and successful. In the conquered lands, no one was forced to give up their faith and become a Muslim. In fact, for 400 years, half of the world's Christians lived in lands ruled by Muslims.

Baghdad's rulers did not tolerate dhimmi just out of kindness. The foreigners' knowledge was valuable, and many of them did unpopular or highly-skilled jobs. Jews, for instance, worked with **molten** metal, making coins. Christians made very good scribes. And there was a price to pay for freedom. Dhimmi had to wear special clothes and pay an extra tax, called "Jizya". This was a kind of protection money through which non-believers bought their safety from **persecution**. Though the very poor were excused, it was a high tax, and some converted to Islam just to avoid it.

Their different clothes and hats show that these travellers are from outside of Baghdad and the villagers welcome them.

41

Educating Europe

The scholars of the House of Wisdom didn't keep their discoveries secret, and gradually, European people began learning of their amazing achievements.

This knowledge trickled into Europe through lands the Arabs had conquered – in particular Sicily, and southern Spain and Portugal. There, the city of Cordoba attracted visitors from all over Europe, who marvelled at the benefits of Arab civilisation – clean, well-lit streets, palaces, hospitals, colleges and libraries.

Amongst those dazzled by Arab knowledge was the French Christian monk, Gerbert of Aurillac. When he became Pope Sylvester II in 999 CE, he encouraged the use of Arabic numbers, and the study of astronomy. In the century that followed, scholars working in Spain translated science books from Arabic into languages Europeans understand.

Interested Europeans also travelled long distances to learn more about Arab science. Eleventh-century English scientist Adelard of Bath spent seven years visiting Greece, Sicily, Turkey and possibly Palestine, returning to translate Arabic versions of important Greek books.

Pope Sylvester II

Finally, Europeans learnt of Arab achievements through warfare. During the **Crusades** at the end of the 11th century, Christian armies **looted** libraries and returned to Europe with the literature and ideas of the House of Wisdom.

Chess was one of the things that Europeans learnt from the Arab world around the time of the Crusades.

Decline and fall
The decline

Soon after its foundation by Al-Manṣūr, Baghdad had spread out from its circular walls until more than a million people lived there. For a while at the end of the 9th century, it was the world's largest city.

However, by 900 CE, Baghdad was already declining. The Abbasid dynasty that ruled the vast Islamic empire had wasted vast sums of money and there were family quarrels. At the beginning of the 9th century, the caliph's own brother challenged his power. In 812 CE, his rebel armies surrounded Baghdad and in a year of bloody fighting, much of the city was destroyed. Some 50 years later, in another civil war, Baghdad was attacked once more, causing further destruction.

The House of Wisdom survived these terrible attacks, but changes of caliph caused greater damage. Al-Mutawakkil, who ruled from 847 CE, didn't have the same respect for knowledge as those who had gone before him. Without royal support, the House of Wisdom withered.

Environmental problems also hurt Baghdad. The rivers that watered Baghdad's surrounding fields contained tiny amounts of salt, but over centuries this collected in the soil, poisoning the crops. Farms could no longer produce enough, and the city's population fell.

Baghdad's fortunes fell further as the Abbasid dynasty weakened. In the 11th century, rival caliphates from Turkey and North Africa invaded and took over the city. Soon after, European Christians challenged the vast Arab empire.

The Crusades

Christians in Europe were unhappy about the spread of Islam: Muslims ruled the Holy Land, where Jesus Christ had lived and died. In 1095, the Pope called on Christians to march to the Holy Land and reconquer it.

The Pope's message led to the Crusades. In the first of these **brutal** religious wars, Christian knights captured the holy city of Jerusalem, killing every Jew and Muslim they found.

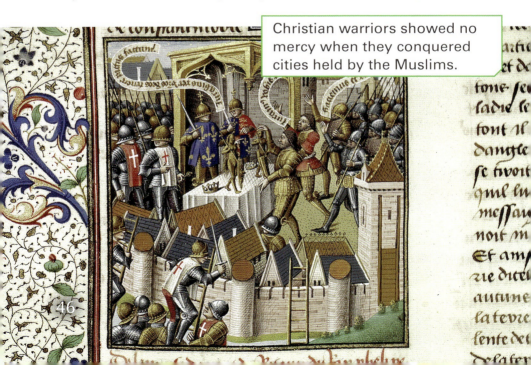

Christian warriors showed no mercy when they conquered cities held by the Muslims.

46

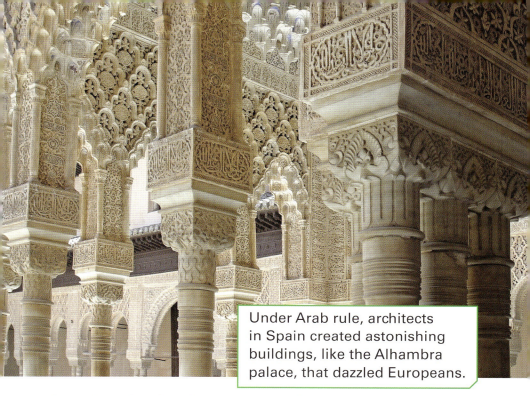

Under Arab rule, architects in Spain created astonishing buildings, like the Alhambra palace, that dazzled Europeans.

But when the slaughter was over, the **conquerors** discovered much to admire in the lands they occupied. Medical care was so good that wounded knights preferred Muslim doctors to Christians. When they returned to Europe, they spread not only Arabic wisdom and learning, but also habits and culture – including new music, perfume, carpets, chess, and **morris dancing**!

Over the next two centuries, more warfare followed, but the Crusaders gradually lost all the land they had conquered. Their victories lasted only in Spain, where in the **Reconquista** they ended Muslim rule in 1492.

Assault from the east

Baghdad's position protected it from attack by the Crusaders: 800 kilometres of desert separated the city from Christian kingdoms on the Mediterranean Sea. But the Crusaders weren't the only threat: Baghdad had enemies to the east. When they attacked, they destroyed the city utterly.

Baghdad's conquerors were Mongol soldiers from China. Under the leadership of Genghis Khan, the Mongol people had built a vast empire that rivalled the Islamic caliphate. Baghdad's defenders had beaten off earlier raids but, in 1258, a vast army of overwhelming power surrounded the city.

Massive catapults demolished Baghdad's walls in less than two weeks, and when the invaders entered the city, they were ruthless. They killed as many as half a million people, piling their hearts in a huge heap.

They didn't spare the scholars of the House of Wisdom or their work. According to legend, the waters of the Tigris ran black with the ink of books from Baghdad's library, and red with blood. Mosques, palaces and hospitals burnt to the ground.

After the destruction, the city was rebuilt, but the canal system that provided water and food was damaged beyond repair. Baghdad didn't regain its former status.

Baghdad in our language and lives

The Mongols destroyed Baghdad, but – fortunately – not before the knowledge of its scholars and the culture of its people had spread across the world. Arabic translation in the House of Wisdom preserved priceless writings from ancient Greece. Original ideas from Arab scientists spread to the capitals of Europe. And the Indian mathematics that would revolutionise calculation travelled through the Islamic world.

The most important result of this transfer of wisdom was the Renaissance – a surge of understanding in art, politics, science and architecture. It began in Italy in the 14th century and spread across Europe.

Today, many of the words we use – from "algebra" to "zero" – remind us of the House of Wisdom and the great Islamic empire. Not all are mathematical: alcohol, admiral, monsoon, cotton and magazine all come from Arabic words.

Admiral Horatio Nelson

The Arab world also introduced us to some of the food we eat. Artichokes, sugar, oranges, apricots and sorbet all have Arabic names.

But the most important reminder comes every time we use numbers. We don't write them like English words, from left to right. Instead we write them like the Arabic language, with the smallest digits on the right, then tens, hundreds, and thousands, farther and farther to the left.

Glossary

allies	countries that have agreed to help one another, particularly during wartime
baffling	difficult to understand
brutal	cruel
calculation	mathematical sum
caliphate	kingdom
complex	complicated, with lots of different pieces
Crusades, the	a series of holy wars
conquered	took control of something by force
conquerors	people who take control of something by force
cultivate	encourage
dynasty	ruling family
enchanted	delighted
Euphrates	the longest river in southwest Asia
exotic	unusual and unfamiliar, coming from far away
fragrance	smell
goods	items for sale such as spices and cloth
hospitality	welcoming someone into your home
infectious	something you might catch easily, for example, a disease
ingenious	very clever
irrigated	watered
loincloth	a piece of material worn around the waist
looted	stole or took by force
manual	a book that tells you how to do something
mercury	a liquid metal
molten	something that melted into liquid
morris dancing	a traditional dance by men wearing bells and holding sticks
mosque	Muslim temple
observatory	a place to watch the night sky
pagans	people who don't follow any particular religion
parched	without water
persecution	mistreatment of a person or group of people
philosopher	thinker and inquirer

prophet	holy man
radically	very different, a new kind of thinking
Reconquista	a Spanish and Portuguese word meaning "reconquest"
Sabeans	people who lived in modern-day Yemen
scholars	people who study a subject in great detail
scholarship	studying at a high level
scribes	professional writers
smallpox	a disease that causes fever and spots on the skin, which can lead to death
sorcerers	people who have magical powers
squalid	dirty and unpleasant
suburbs	areas with lots of houses
symptoms	signs, such as spots or a cough, that might mean you have a disease
Zoroastrians	followers of the Iranian religion Zoroastrianism

Index

The greatest city in the world

Learning

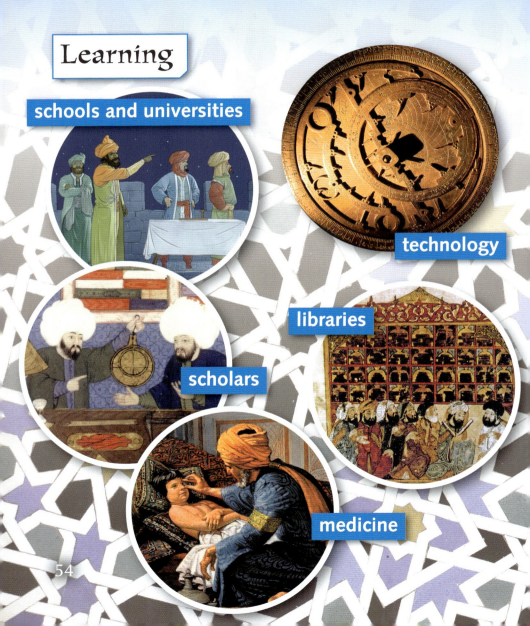

schools and universities

technology

libraries

scholars

medicine

Ideas for reading

Written by Clare Dowdall, PhD
Lecturer and Primary Literacy Consultant

Reading objectives:
- make comparisons within and across books
- discuss understanding and explore the meaning of words in context
- retrieve, record and present information from non-fiction
- explain and discuss their understanding of what they have read, including through formal presentations and debates, maintaining a focus on the topic and using notes where necessary

Spoken language objectives:
- ask relevant questions to extend their understanding and knowledge
- participate in discussions, presentations, performances, role play, improvisations and debates

Curriculum links: History – non-European study (Baghdad)

Resources: whiteboards, pens and paper, ICT for research, drawing materials, rulers and card for making geometric shape templates

Build a context for reading
- Help children to read the word "Baghdad".
- Look at the image on the front cover. Ask children to describe what they can see and to suggest what is meant by the phrase "Golden Age".
- Read the blurb and discuss where the city of Baghdad is. Ask children what they can infer and deduce from the information in the blurb, and collect their ideas on a whiteboard.

Understand and apply reading strategies
- Read pp2–3 aloud, asking children to listen for three key facts about Baghdad. Share their ideas together.
- Ask children to reread pp2–3 with a partner, looking for information about how Baghdad and European cities compared. Challenge pairs to recount their findings.

Building

houses

mosques

gardens

palaces

Living

jobs

rich

poor

55